# MARK TWAIN

*A Life From Beginning to End*

Copyright © 2018 by Hourly History.

All rights reserved.

# Table of Contents

Introduction
The Mississippi Steamboat Pilot
Westward to Fame and Fortune
The Short-lived Sunlight
Tom Sawyer and Huckleberry Finn
Debts and Bankruptcy
Family Travels and Deaths
The Last Years
Conclusion

# Introduction

"The average American loves his family," wrote Thomas Edison. "If he has any love left over for some other person, he generally selects Mark Twain." Mark Twain, the beloved author who gave voice to the unique place that was and is the United States, was also Samuel Clemens. Clemens lived an adventurous, wandering life, beginning with his travels to the West as a young man and ending with his retreat to Bermuda in his final months. His boyhood in Hannibal, Missouri and time piloting a steamboat on the Mississippi would later reappear in some of Twain's most famous works, *The Adventures of Tom Sawyer* and *The Adventures of Huckleberry Finn*.

Though Twain became known first as a humorist, Clemens' life was marked by tragedy. Clemens spent much of his life seeking prosperity only to see it disappear and to have to work his way out from under massive debts. He loved his wife, Livy—a woman whom society declared inaccessible to him, but whom he convinced to marry him anyway—and his three daughters, yet also saw them leave his life, as Livy and two of their daughters died before Clemens. Despite these crushing blows, he carried on writing—in fact, his writing and his increasingly dark sense of humor were what helped him keep going through grief and depression.

In this book, you will meet both Samuel Clemens and Mark Twain, the man and the author. Discover the life of the man who through many difficulties succeeded in becoming a voice for a young nation—a voice that still rings true for many readers today and has helped define American literature.

# Chapter One

# The Mississippi Steamboat Pilot

*"When I was a boy, there was but one permanent ambition among my comrades in our village on the west bank of the Mississippi River. That was, to be a steamboatman."*

—Mark Twain, Life on the Mississippi

In a small shack in the tiny village of Florida, Missouri, Samuel Clemens was born on November 30, 1835. His father, John Marshall Clemens, was a stern man whom Samuel—later to become known as Mark Twain—could not remember ever laughing. John, originally from Virginia, had moved westward time and time again seeking success. Samuel's mother Jane, on the other hand, was enthusiastic and eloquent, enjoying community events, dancing, and storytelling as well as the many cats she took in. The Clemens family would grow to include seven children, though only four would live to adulthood. Samuel was the sixth and was small and sickly, soon earning him the nickname "Little Sammy."

In 1839, the family packed up and moved away from the failing settlement of Florida. They resettled 35 miles to the northwest, in Hannibal, Missouri. Later on, this town would provide a backdrop for some of Mark Twain's most famous stories. John Clemens bought the Virginia House, a hotel, but the business soon failed when the town did not grow fast enough to supply a steady stream of guests. Money troubles intensified for the family when John's second attempt at a business, a dry-goods store, also collapsed. At last, John sent Orion, his oldest son, to St. Louis, where Orion would help support the family by learning to become a printer.

The difficulties of Samuel's childhood included the deaths of two siblings and a move from the house John had built on Hill Street to a smaller apartment, necessary because of debt. Despite these things, Sam's remembrance of his life in Hannibal was positive; he later called the town "a boy's paradise." He had friends with whom to explore the nearby woods and the Mississippi River. They swam, fished, smoked corncob pipes, and spent time playing on an island. Several times, Sam came near drowning. They spent days imagining themselves to be Indians or gold-seekers or pirates and came up with pranks to play in town.

Sam read avidly, absorbing books like *The Arabian Nights* and *Robinson Crusoe*. But he was not a particularly good student in any other way. He was always energetic and preferred to be out of school, sometimes skipping school and once trying to run away by hiding on a steamboat. He was also no fan of church; he often failed to attend the evening services that his mother sent him to, memorizing Bible verses on his own so that he could pretend he had gone. Among his best friends was Tom

Blankenship, the son of Hannibal's drunkard. Though Sam was not allowed to spend time with Tom, he would often sneak out at night to meet his friend.

Sam's childhood in Missouri introduced him to slavery, as well. He spent part of each summer at his uncle's farm, where he got to know the 30 slaves. From Mary Quarles, a girl his own age who became his friend on the farm, to Uncle Dan'l, who introduced Sam to the sound of spirituals and told ghost stories, Sam found himself drawn to these African-Americans. As a boy, he did not yet think of slavery as wrong, though he had many other opportunities to observe it. His father bought and sold some slaves as well as owning a slave girl named Jennie. He also vividly recalled the miserable faces of slaves chained together, waiting to be sent to New Orleans.

By the time Sam Clemens turned 12, his life had taken an unexpected turn. Earlier in the year, his father campaigned to be the clerk of the county court—a position that would finally offer him the success he'd been seeking, and one that he seemed likely to win. But just before the election, he caught pneumonia and soon died. The money from Orion was not enough to support the family, so Sam's mother began to accept boarders, and his sister gave piano lessons. Though Sam had three more years of schooling after his father's death, he too worked after school and in the summers—though in his own words, he worked "not diligently, not willingly, but fretfully, lazily, repiningly, complainingly, disgustedly, and always shirking the work when I was not watched." At last, he needed to leave school and these temporary jobs to enter into an apprenticeship as a printer for the *Missouri Courier*. In return, he was paid with his board and a set of ill-fitting clothes each year.

When Orion returned to Hannibal and bought the *Hannibal Journal,* Sam went to work for him. Orion was energetic, restless, changeable, and not a very good businessman, and even though Sam worked for him for two years, Orion could never pay him the weekly salary that they had agreed upon. Working for the *Hannibal Journal* did give Sam the chance to begin writing—he mainly produced humorous pieces such as character sketches and light verse, all printed under the pen name W. Epaminondas Adrastus Blab. He once got himself in trouble by printing sketches of the town's leaders when Orion was gone and left him in charge.

Work for the *Hannibal Journal*—and the town of Hannibal itself—had begun to feel too small to Sam by the time he turned 17. With a promise to his mother that he would avoid smoking and drinking, Sam left Hannibal in 1853. He moved first to St. Louis and, with his printing experience, found a job with the *Evening News*. With the little bit of money he earned there, he was soon off to a new place. He took a train for the first time in his life, heading to New York City where he would find work in a print shop. This gave him an income of four dollars per week and the chance to read many books. Before long, however, he set out once again. He moved to Philadelphia and then Washington, D.C.

In 1854, a year after setting out from home, Sam was ready to leave the East. Jane Clemens and Sam's younger brother, Henry, had left Hannibal and now lived near Orion in Keokuk, Iowa, so Sam went there and joined Orion at his print shop. Orion, now married, had not improved as a manager and businessman, and it soon became evident that he would not be able to pay Sam a salary now any more than he had before. So Sam began to earn money through his writing for the first time, writing travel letters for the *Keokuk Post* using the name Thomas Jefferson Snodgrass. Before long, the man who would become a perpetual wanderer was, not surprisingly, on the move again. He returned to St. Louis and then moved to Chicago and Cincinnati.

When he was 21, Sam set out for New Orleans; he intended to go all the way to Brazil where he wanted to join the growing trade in cocoa plants. But he would not make it that far. Traveling by steamboat reawakened the dream of his boyhood of making a living on the river, and he convinced the pilot of the *Paul Jones*, the steamboat on which he was a passenger, to train him as a steamboat pilot. The pilot, Horace Bixby, agreed to this arrangement in exchange for $500 of Sam Clemens' future wages.

Sam soon learned how demanding and difficult piloting a steamboat on the Mississippi could be. The task required that he know both landmarks along the river and the river itself—how to read the current and ripples of the surface to avoid hidden reefs, navigate through fallen trees, and find safe channels through the constantly changing waterway. He needed to interpret the depths of the river as the leadsmen called it out using terms such as "quarter-twain," "half-twain," and "mark twain"—the call that indicated a safe depth. He had to do this no matter the weather or time of day or night, continually making decisions that affected the safety of the boat, cargo, and passengers.

When Orion's print shop collapsed and Sam's younger brother Henry needed a new job, Sam suggested he look for work on the river as well. Sam had switched to a steamboat named the *Pennsylvania*, and he helped Henry get a job as the boat's clerk. Before they set out, Sam had an upsetting dream where he saw Henry dressed in one of Sam's suits, laid out in a metal coffin with white roses and one red rose. Soon Sam, still a cub pilot, had a quarrel with the boat's chief pilot and had to move to another boat, the *A.T. Lacey*; he and Henry intended to reconvene in St. Louis.

This plan was interrupted by tragedy. Passing Greenville, Mississippi, Sam heard rumors that the *Pennsylvania*'s boilers had exploded and the boat had sunk, resulting in mass casualties. News from the papers was contradictory on whether Henry was safe or not, and the *A.T. Lacey*, just two days behind the *Pennsylvania*, passed bodies in the water at the site of the explosion. When the *A.T. Lacey* arrived in Memphis, Sam hurried to the temporary hospital where he found Henry among the injured, terribly burned. Henry had been thrown from the boat in the explosion but had gone back to help others and was consequently caught in a second explosion.

He was not expected to survive, and Sam stayed beside his brother for days until Henry woke in great pain. As a doctor had instructed him, Sam asked for morphine for Henry, but the young doctor who provided it had no way to measure the dose and may have given Henry too much. Henry soon fell asleep again and then died. Sam blamed himself, both for not being with Henry on the steamer and for asking for morphine for his brother. Strangely, Sam's dream came true to the last detail: the women of Memphis raised money to buy Henry a special metal coffin instead of the usual pine, Henry had to be dressed in Sam's clothes, and an old woman laid a bouquet of white roses with one red rose on Henry's chest.

Despite this haunting personal tragedy, Sam received his pilot's certificate in 1859. It was his ticket to a secure income, more than his father or older brother had ever earned. Sam relished the independent life of a steamboat pilot, who answered to no one once on the river, not even the captain. He later wrote, "I loved the profession far better than any I have followed since, and I took measureless pride in it." He worked on 18 different steamboats, having a wide variety of opportunities to observe the people and places around him; he also continued to write, producing satirical pieces for newspapers. Samuel Clemens felt that he had found his future on the river, and he expected to work as a pilot for the rest of his life. But tensions in the United States were rising, and in 1861, the Civil War broke out—a war that put a halt to commercial traffic on the Mississippi. During Sam's last trip as a pilot, a Union shell broke the glass of the boat's pilothouse. Arriving in St. Louis, Sam's job as a steamboat pilot was over, and he now needed a new direction.

# Chapter Two

# Westward to Fame and Fortune

*"Everybody knows me, & I fare like a prince wherever I go, be it on this side of the mountains or the other. And I am proud to say I am the most conceited ass in the Territory."*

—Mark Twain, letter to his mother

Sam did not take a strong side as the war began—Orion had been part of Lincoln's campaign, but his mother, on the other hand, hated the "Yankees" of the North. For his part, Sam wanted to return to work on the Mississippi, and so he hoped for the war to end quickly. Bored, Sam returned to Hannibal and for a few weeks joined a Confederate militia organized by some of his boyhood friends. Before long, most of the young men left the small militia to join the actual Confederate army. Sam had no interest in this, however, and began to look towards the West, instead. Orion, through connections made during Lincoln's campaign, had been appointed as the secretary of the newly-formed Territory of Nevada. Sam intended to travel westward with his brother and even offered to pay for their stagecoach tickets to be allowed to come along—a total cost of $300.

In the summer of 1861, Orion and Sam boarded the stagecoach in St. Joseph, Missouri. Despite the strict weight limit for their luggage, Orion brought a stack of law books and a full dictionary. For three weeks, the brothers journeyed towards Carson City. Sam was delighted by the trip, seeing new animals like jackrabbits and buffalo and marveling at snow in the summer as they crossed the mountains. He met Native Americans and an outlaw and spotted a Pony Express rider. On hot days, he rode on the roof of the stage in his underwear.

As Orion took up his work as secretary of the territory, Sam was left to find a path for himself. His first adventure was to explore the Lake Tahoe area with a friend. Not only was he impressed by the lake's beauty, but he and his friend saw financial potential in the timber nearby and staked several claims. Unfortunately for their dreams, it was just a few days before Sam let a campfire get out of control and their timber claims burned in the ensuing forest fire. Next, Sam joined the many men who had succumbed to "silver fever," searching the hills of Nevada for silver and staking various claims for half a year. He ended this unsuccessful venture in the fall of 1862, in debt but still dreaming of making his fortune in the West. In a letter back home, he wrote, "My livelihood must be made in this country—and if I have to wait longer than I expected, let it be so—I have no fear of failure."

But despite this air of self-confidence, Sam had no idea what to do next. He had held many short-term jobs, but except in his work as a steamboat pilot, he never felt that he excelled. But soon an unexpected opportunity arose. Sam had written a number of pieces to the *Territorial Enterprise,* Nevada's first newspaper, when he was still pursuing mining. Now that he had given up his endeavors in that field, the newspaper offered him full-time work. As a reporter, he once again found a task he loved to do. He enjoyed hunting down news throughout Virginia City, from the police station to the saloons. He had no qualms about making up news stories—often humorous but sometimes mistaken for truth. His salary soon grew from $25 a week to $6 a day. With his reputation growing even faster than his salary, in February of 1863, Sam Clemens took up a new pen name: Mark Twain.

Mark Twain's fame soon spread, and by the next year, his articles were common in California and even sometimes spotted in Eastern papers. He used his new name not only for the newspaper but sometimes for his letters home; even some of his friends began to call him Mark. For the rest of this book, he will be referred to as Mark Twain even though his legal name, Samuel Clemens, would remain unchanged.

In spite of his fame, the restlessness of his youth soon caught up to Twain again. He felt he needed change and took the opportunity to leave the territory when one of his rival reporters seemed on the verge of challenging him to a duel. His escape took him even further west, to San Francisco. He enjoyed relative wealth and fame there, associating with other well-known writers while working for a newspaper called the *Morning Calling* as well as occasionally writing for literary journals.

He had counted on his collection of mining stocks for future wealth, planning to sell them when the mining boom came; when it did, he missed it and found himself nearly out of money. After disagreements with his editor, he also lost his job at the *Morning Call*. He spent two more miserable months in San Francisco, avoiding the acquaintances of his more fortunate days.

When a friend, Jim Gillis, invited him out to the Sierras to visit mining camps, Twain accepted. Though he spent much of the time waiting out the rain and eating, as he wrote in his journal, "beans and dishwater," one of the most valuable moments of his career arrived as he sat around a fire with a group of miners. There, he heard a story that he re-spun as "The Celebrated Jumping Frog of Calaveras County." He sent the story to Artemus Ward, the foremost humorist in America at the time, whom Twain had met previously when Ward passed through Virginia City.

When Twain made his way back to San Francisco soon after, he was considering going back East—the Civil War had finally ended—but he was ashamed of his failures. He was jailed for public drunkenness and came close to committing suicide. Luckily, good news was on its way.

Artemus Ward had sent Twain's story to the *New York Saturday Press* . It became a sensation, with many other papers reprinting it and praising the author. Twain made light of this success, but it nonetheless encouraged him, and in 1866 he headed off for Honolulu with a commission to write humorous travel letters for the *Sacramento Union*. He remained in Hawaii for four months, exploring sugar plantations and volcanic craters, documenting his travels in letters that quickly achieved popularity back in California. He capitalized on this when he returned through a series of lectures—despite his initial nervousness, his humorous talks were hugely successful, and he found himself well-paid and in high demand. Now that he had at last found fame and a measure of fortune in the West, Mark Twain set his sights on a new goal—New York City.

## Chapter Three

# The Short-lived Sunlight

*"She is the most perfect gem of womankind that ever I saw in my life—& will stand by that remark until I die."*

—Mark Twain, letter to Will Bowen

New York, where Mark Twain found himself in 1867, was expensive and crowded. Here he was not an acclaimed writer and speaker, but another man among a million. He was collecting material to write travel letters for the *Alta California*, and he did his work well, exploring all the city had to offer—from churches, theatres, and museums, to dirty and crowded tenements. He took a short trip to the Midwest to repeat his success as a lecturer.

In May, his first book, *The Celebrated Jumping Frog of Calaveras County, and Other Sketches,* was published with a dedication to his mother. The book did not sell well, however, and Twain was troubled to think how little help he had been able to bring to his family in all his wanderings. He felt alone in the huge city and began to think that the time had come to take to the road again.

In June, he left for Europe on a trip funded by the *Alta California* and two papers in New York. He traveled aboard the *Quaker City*, a steamship that would spend five months journeying across the Atlantic, through the

Mediterranean, and finally to the Holy Land. Many of the passengers were pious Midwesterners whom Mark Twain viewed with a hearty dose of skepticism. He still participated in shipboard events, such as prayer services, a choir, a debate club, and games like shuffleboard. At the same time, he collected a group of men who would meet in his cabin at night to drink, smoke, and play cards. While his fellow travelers saw him as "the Wild Humorist of the Pacific Slope," Twain welcomed the help of a Cleveland publisher's wife, Mary Mason Fairbanks, who tried to teach him how to fit into polite Eastern society.

As the tour moved from Gibraltar to the highlights of Italy, Mark Twain recorded what he saw. The *Quaker City* passed Athens, where a cholera outbreak meant that passengers were supposed to be quarantined on the ship—but Twain and his friends sneaked into the city at night anyways—and then on to Constantinople (modern-day Istanbul). Upon their arrival in Beirut in September, Twain and his friends chose to leave the ship and make their way forward by pack train, an adventure during which he described events such as a camel's attempt to eat his overcoat and manuscript. The friends saw sites mentioned in the Bible such as Jericho and Bethlehem, and at last found themselves in Jerusalem. From there, the *Quaker City* took them to Egypt to visit the Great Pyramid and the Sphinx.

Throughout, Mark Twain's account of his travels was unique in that he did not portray Europe as some kind of unreachable and superior standard or the Holy Land and Egypt as completely exotic and strange, but instead made comparisons with American scenes and sometimes made fun of what he saw. He also poked fun at the other passengers, laughing at the habits and fashions taken on by Americans who had traveled to Europe.

Twain returned to New York in November with intentions of increasing his fame. For a while, he worked at different jobs—he served as secretary to a Nevada senator, resumed his lecturing tours by heading westward, and even tried to become postmaster of San Francisco until he learned how little he would be paid in that position.

The following year, 1868, brought change to Twain's life when he went to visit one of his friends from the *Quaker City*, Charley Langdon, in Elmira, New York. He had met Charley's sister Olivia several times before and wanted to get to know her more. The Langdons introduced Twain to life as he had never seen it before. Not only were they quite wealthy, but they were a family who affectionately showed love to one another. They also were adamantly against slavery—the family had helped runaway slaves on their way north. And they did not drink anything more alcoholic than apple cider.

Olivia Langdon, often called Livy, was well-educated, beautiful, fervently religious, delicate in health, and ten years younger than Twain. He quickly fell in love with her, and it did not take him long to tell her so. She rejected him, only conceding that they could write letters, but must do so as brother and sister and her letters must be addressed to Charley to keep rumors from spreading. This was the beginning of a 17-month exchange, during which

Twain sent Livy 184 letters. Livy had no hesitations about correcting Twain or trying to improve his character. At one point, he nearly gave up hope, but then received a letter including a picture of Livy.

As he tried to woo Livy by post, Twain was busy touring and giving lectures again, talking about his journey on the *Quaker City*. In the late fall of 1868, he spoke in Elmira and saw the Langdons. Though Livy turned Twain down twice more, finally she agreed to marry him. Her father was shocked and insisted that Twain acquire letters of reference from friends in the West. When these letters arrived, their descriptions of Twain did little to assuage Jervis Langdon's concerns, though they hardly differed from what Twain had already said of himself. Livy, for her part, was determined to reform Twain, sending him sermons and making him promise to give up swearing and drinking. At last Jervis agreed to the couple's engagement, but Twain still needed to find a steady source of income that did not require him to travel constantly.

Twain refused Jervis's offer to get involved in the family coal business, but with a loan from his future father-in-law, he was able to purchase the *Buffalo Express*. Consequently, Twain began to travel between Buffalo, Montana, and Elmira. In Elmira, Livy helped Twain edit his expanded account of his time traveling on the *Quaker City*. This was published in 1869 by the American Publishing Company of Hartford, Connecticut as *The Innocents Abroad*. His book not only became popular with general readers but also received some positive reviews from critics, compelling Twain to begin work on an account of his adventures in the West that would become *Roughing It.*

In February of 1870, Twain and Livy were married. Then the couple, the Langdons, and several friends immediately left by train for Buffalo. There, Jervis surprised Twain with the gift of a large, well-furnished, and fully staffed house. The couple was happy during the following months as they began their lives together, writing of their joy in joint letters to family and friends. Livy wrote, "We are two as happy people as you ever saw. Our days seem to be made up of only bright sunlight with no shadow in them." Livy's questions and affection helped Twain to begin thinking about his past and childhood, memories that would become important in his later writings.

But the days of "bright sunlight with no shadow" were to be short-lived, as death and sickness invaded their lives. Jervis Langdon died of cancer six months after his daughter's wedding. Livy's best friend died while visiting the couple in Buffalo to help Livy cope with the loss of her father. Then Livy, who was also pregnant, came down with typhoid. She lived, but barely, and her baby was born prematurely and weighed only just over four pounds.

Twain, writing in a letter that "I had rather die twice over than repeat the last six months of my life," decided to sell the house and the *Buffalo Express* and move his family east to Hartford, Connecticut. This move brought financial difficulties and debt, and Twain had to do another series of lectures to make ends meet. After five months of exhausting traveling, he was able to return to Hartford. There, in March of 1872, Livy gave birth to a second child, a daughter named Olivia Susan, whom the family would call Susy. By this time, profits from *The Innocents Abroad* began to help the family's financial situation.

However, the dark times were not over. Barely two months after Susy's birth, Twain and Livy's first child died. Livy's grief for her son added to her grief over her father's death, while Twain felt guilt, just as he had with his brothers' deaths years earlier. Livy's strong religious faith began to waver as she felt, as she recorded, "so often as if my path is to be lined with graves." She no longer wanted to go to church. For this change in Livy, too, Twain felt responsible.

# Chapter Four

# Tom Sawyer and Huckleberry Finn

*"He is a very good man and a very funny one. He has got a temper, but we all of us have in this family . . . He is known to the public as a humorist, but he has much more in him that is earnest than humorous."*

—Susy Clemens, at age 13, on her father, Samuel Clemens (Mark Twain)

Despite the difficulties of the early years of Twain and Livy's marriage and the move to Hartford, better times were coming. Mark Twain left for England soon after his son's death, planning to collect new material for another book. Instead, he found England beautiful and discovered he did not want to satirize the country when he still saw so much room for satire about his own country. The next year, in the summer, he returned to England again with his family. There he met many famous British authors, such as Lewis Carroll.

Back home in the United States, Twain started work on a new book, *The Gilded Age*. This book told the story of Eschol Sellers, a man whose motto is "There's millions in it" as he constantly dreams of the next way to get rich.

Twain recorded that the character, who would later appear in a play and another novel, was based on his cousin. But Twain soon realized that he was, himself, much like Colonel Sellers—both constantly searching for greater wealth and displaying his wealth in his style of living.

One of Twain's methods of pursuing this display of prosperity was through the construction of a new house in 1874. The house was not only huge, with 19 rooms, but was also unique—even odd—in its design. Later on, viewers hypothesized that the house was meant to resemble the Mississippi steamboats of Twain's youth; while this idea had not actually been the inspiration for the house's design, Twain enjoyed the comparison.

The year of 1874 also marked the birth of Twain and Livy's second daughter, Clara, along with the first of about 20 summers that the family would spend near Elmira on Quarry Farm. Susan Langdon Crane, an adopted sister of Livy's, lived on the farm. She provided a quiet pavilion on a hill for Twain's writing, where he spent many happy days working furiously while smoking his Wheeling "long nine" cigars. It was here, in 1874, that Mark Twain began drawing on memories of his childhood in Hannibal to write *The Adventures of Tom Sawyer*, the book that would become the most popular of all his works.

Once the family moved into their house in the fall, their family life began to take a more defined shape. Twain enjoyed pretending to be animals with his two daughters in the library and reading aloud to them. He also made up stories for them. The family celebrated Christmas lavishly, and Twain sometimes even dressed up as St. Nicholas. Livy remained ill but did her best to supervise the servants, keep track of financial matters, and keep the household running smoothly even during Twain's travels. Twain had frequent mood swings and an explosive temper, yet his daughters still loved him. Despite their differences, Twain and Livy also loved one another sincerely throughout their lives.

In the summer of 1876, at Quarry Farm once again, Twain began work on another book. This one would become *The Adventures of Huckleberry Finn*. Though *Huckleberry Finn* again drew on Twain's boyhood memories, as *Tom Sawyer* had done, this second book delved much more deeply into the situation of the United States and the continuing oppression of the new-freed African-Americans. Issues of slavery and race rise to the surface of the novel, as Huck Finn runs away, floating a raft down the Mississippi with an escaped slave named Jim. Huck, having grown up in a society that taught him that slavery is right and that it is his moral duty to report Jim's escape, comes to questions what he knows about good and evil as he gets to know Jim. The writing of the novel was not smooth sailing for Twain, however, who was uncertain if he would ever want to publish it and gave up work on it at the end of the summer.

He soon began work on other books: *1601* and *A Tramp Abroad*, the latter based on a 17-month trip through Europe with his family. Twain and Livy's third daughter, Jean, was born in 1880. The following year,

Twain wrote a children's book called *The Prince and the Pauper*, an attempt to produce something different from his usual humor and prove his ability to write in a more literary style. Livy and the girls loved the book, with Susy even declaring, "It is unquestionably the best book he has ever written." She believed that the book showed more of her father's true character than his usual humorous writings did; it showed "his kind sympathetic nature" that few saw. Critics also celebrated Twain's use of language in *The Prince and the Pauper*, and Twain himself was pleased with the book.

In the spring of 1882, Twain visited the Mississippi again with a steamboat trip from St. Louis to New Orleans. He found that the river's course had changed so much that he could no longer recognize where he was, but he enjoyed the landscape and the chance to see old friends. This return to the South inspired him to begin work on *Huckleberry Finn* again during the summer. He worked intensely, shaping the story that would finally be published in its complete form in 1885, by Twain's newly formed publishing company, Charles L. Webster & Co.

Along the way, Livy helped Twain revise and edit the manuscript, removing the most objectionable pieces. The story was serialized in *The Century* magazine, and the magazine's editor also made changes. Despite this, the book still received criticism and was denounced by *Life* magazine, as well as author Louisa May Alcott, as not suitable for children. It was soon banned from the library of Concord, Massachusetts—an event that Clemens at least claimed to be pleased about, expecting that it would increase sales.

At the same time, the former U.S. president Ulysses S. Grant, whom Twain had become friends with, discovered that his business partner had cheated him and left their banking firm with no assets. The former president, now financially ruined, took Twain's offer to publish his autobiography. Grant began writing and continued despite developing throat cancer and losing his ability to speak. He finished his last revisions in July of 1885—just days before his death—and consequently, the autobiography was immediately in high demand. For Twain, Grant's *Memoirs* were a great success, adding to his prosperity.

Mark Twain wrote around this time, "It seems to me that whatever I touch turns to gold," and he claimed that he was "thoroughly and unceasingly happy." His family lived in luxury, and the dinners they gave were lavish affairs—even if Livy Clemens had to work out a series of phrases in code to help Twain regulate his behavior. Twain enjoyed performing the spirituals that he had learned in his boyhood from Uncle Dan'l, and his daughters developed performances as well.

The year after he published *Huckleberry Finn*, Twain began on his next novel, *A Connecticut Yankee in King Arthur's Court*. The book did not receive good reviews, but Twain believed that he had found another way to make money and that he was done with writing. His publishing company was doing well now that he had published Grant's *Memoirs*, and he was expanding his business by signing up other famous people to write their autobiographies. He invested in stocks, as well, though he frequently lost money with this speculation. He stayed on the forefront of new technology, using a typewriter and installing a telephone despite the fact that he struggled with typing on the typewriter, which he said made him "want to swear," and that the telephone was unreliable.

He invested huge amounts of money in other technology as well, from a steam generator to a marine telegraph. These investments did not make a profit, nor did two out of the three of Twain's own patented inventions. He was fascinated with the new, the cutting-edge, and with discovery itself. But at the top of the list was a machine that a Hartford machinist named James W. Paige was working to invent. Paige intended this machine to simplify the typesetting process and change the entire printing industry. Twain believed whole-heartedly in the promises that Paige made, and he continued to sink money into the machine for years, even as his publishing company began to fail. He even borrowed against his savings to fund Paige's efforts, encouraged by each development. Paige continued to insist on making modifications and improvements to the machine.

At last, in early 1891, Twain gave up his hopes of obtaining riches through Paige's invention. He and his family were left in difficult financial straits, and it was up to the writings of Mark Twain to provide for the Clemens family once again.

# Chapter Five

# Debts and Bankruptcy

*"The billows of hell have been rolling over me. A body forgets pretty much everything, these days, except his visions of the poorhouse."*

—Mark Twain, 1891 letter

Twain turned out another book, *The American Claimant*, within just a few months. However, he was suffering from rheumatism that gave him severe pain in his writing arm. Livy, too, was still suffering from health issues—rheumatism and some kind of heart trouble. Doctors suggested that the best solution for her health would be a period of rest far away from home, in Europe. Twain, though he found he no longer wanted to travel, did see the financial sense of closing up the massive and expensive house in Hartford. On top of this, traveling in Europe would give him new opportunities for travel writing, his old standby.

By the time spring of 1891 ended, the family was packed and ready to leave. Twain was not the only family member feeling unenthusiastic about the journey—his daughters and Livy were also sad to leave their house, community, friends, and pets. Nonetheless, the family was soon on their way. They would spend the summer and fall traveling through France, Switzerland, and Germany.

While his family enjoyed their travels, Twain said that he felt continually out of place. He was still having difficulty with his arm when he wrote, and his financial situation brought him continual stress. He told a friend that "I have never felt so desperate in all my life." Still, he was well known throughout Europe and hailed as a celebrity wherever he went, even dining with Kaiser Wilhelm II.

At the end of the summer, the family settled down for a time near Florence, Italy. Florence suited Livy's health, which continually improved. Twain's arm also began to feel better, and he was able to write consistently again, working on two books: *Tom Sawyer Abroad* and *Pudd'nhead Wilson*.

Despite these positives, complications were quickly arising within the Clemens family as Twain and Livy's daughters grew older. Twain was disturbed during this time in Florence to realize that his daughters, while admiring him, had also always been afraid of his temper and fluctuating moods. By this time, Susy was 19; she had studied for a year at Bryn Mawr before her parents recalled her to join them on their trip to Europe. She began to find the routines of her tight-knit family constraining and boring. Clara went to Berlin alone to pursue her interests in music, but when she returned to Florence, a visit from a young officer caused Twain to lock her in her room for days.

Additionally, even with Twain's steady writing, the debts of his publishing company still weighed down the family's finances. By 1893, he decided he needed to return to America, both to deal with the publishing company and to see if anything could be done with the typesetting machine in which he had invested so much money. This would be the first of eight journeys back and forth between his family in the Old World and his business affairs in the New—journeys which necessitated a separation that both he and Livy found lonely and exhausting.

Twain kept up his hopes that something might come of the machine investment and that he might be able to work out the troubles of his publishing business until the economic crash that followed the Panic of 1893 hit. Now creditors were calling in the publishing company's debts, and he could find no new loans. Twain's health suffered as he stayed up late at night trying to total his debts and make ends meet. Beyond this, his older brother Orion, nearly 70, could not get a job and needed Twain's support. Twain was more desperate than ever before, seeing before him not only his own failures but also the eerie shadow of his father's legacy of not being able to find the prosperity he sought to provide for his family.

It was at this moment that Henry Huttleston Rogers entered Mark Twain's life. Rogers was the founder and vice president of Standard Oil, a ruthless and unapologetic capitalist of the type Twain had satirized in his writings, yet he was an admirer of Mark Twain's books. When he offered Twain both a loan for the publishing business and his personal help in evaluating his business and financial situation, Twain accepted.

Rogers told Twain to stop worrying, but even the successful businessman found Twain's affairs difficult to sort out. At last, in 1894, he convinced Twain that the publishing company would need to declare bankruptcy—a humiliating blow to the family. But with Rogers' help, they retained Twain's copyrights and the house in Hartford, due to Livy's investment of her inheritance in both. Rogers also found a newspaper willing to test the typesetting machine; Twain had high hopes that at last he would receive a return on his massive investment, but the machine proved to be unreliable and unpractical, destroying the family's hopes of returning to Hartford.

Twain still managed to finish another book during this time, *Personal Recollections of Joan of Arc*. He later explained that he based his image of Joan of Arc on Susy, and both he and his family considered the book to be his best work. But one more book could not dig him out of the financial hole in which he found himself, especially as, on the advice of Rogers and Livy, he had promised to pay back his creditors despite his bankruptcy to maintain his reputation. Consequently, he turned to the one sure money-making scheme to which he had hoped never to return—he decided to do another lecture tour. This tour would take him not only across the U.S. but also around the world to five continents.

## Chapter Six

# Family Travels and Deaths

*"I have spent the day alone—thinking; sometimes bitter thoughts, sometimes only sad ones. Reproaching myself for laying the foundations of all our troubles . . . Reproaching myself for a million things whereby I have brought misfortune and sorrow to this family."*

—Mark Twain, 1896 letter to Livy

Twain's daughters were horrified that he would have to return to being seen merely as Mark Twain, the humorist, but Livy and Clara still insisted that they would come along with him. Susy and Jean would stay near Elmira with their aunt Susan Crane, where Jean could go to school. The family hoped that after a year they could be reunited. Twain, Livy, and Clara set off on the first stage of the journey, visiting 22 cities in only a month as they made their way towards Vancouver. Despite a carbuncle on his leg that constantly pained him and made walking difficult, Twain gave his lectures and sent $5,000 back to Rogers to begin paying off his debts.

They next traveled on to Hawaii, where a quarantine stopped them from going ashore, much to Twain's disappointment. Fiji, Australia, and New Zealand next welcomed them. Everywhere they were greeted enthusiastically and found crowds who seemed to have large portions of Mark Twain's work committed to memory. His performances were consistently sold out. Recurrences of his painful carbuncle did not stop Twain as he headed on to Ceylon and India and celebrated his 60th birthday along the way. He kept careful notes as he traveled, intending to write another travel book upon his return.

During the three months he spent in India, Twain was impressed by the Taj Mahal and the height of the Himalayas, though he kept up his old pattern of comparing and criticizing sights abroad in relation to those back home; he claimed that the Taj Mahal was not quite as beautiful as the trees in Hartford coated in ice and that the Himalayas were too tall to be agreeable. He was, however, interested in the cobras, monkeys, and elephants he encountered, describing the excellence of an elephant as a vehicle.

The tour next took the family to the continent of Africa, where Twain found himself disgusted by the self-righteousness he saw in the imperialism of his day. What he had observed, not only in Africa but also India and Australia, reminded him of the slavery he had seen during his childhood. He wrote bitterly of his own race's treatment of other races, commenting, "there are many humorous things in the world; among them the white man's notion that he is less savage than the other savages."

At last he, Livy, and Clara boarded a ship bound for England, their last stop before returning home to the United States. Twain was exhausted and ready to be done with lecturing, despite the appearances planned for England and the likely prospect of yet another tour afterward. He had made significant progress toward paying off his debts, and he was also planning to turn his travel notes into a book called *Following the Equator*. Susy and Jean were supposed to meet the rest of the family in England, and they all looked forward to being together once again.

But bad news soon arrived. Susy had a serious fever, and the two young women's journey to England had to be postponed. A telegram assured the family that Susy would recover, though it would take some time. Livy and Clara set off immediately to be with Susy in the U.S. while Twain began to search for a place for his family to stay in England when they all arrived.

Just three days after Livy and Clara boarded the steamer for America, a telegram informed Twain that Susy had died. She had spent the summer with friends in Hartford, known for playing the piano and singing in the family's old home—performances that drew neighbors to the windows to listen. The fever had come on suddenly, and Susy had not wanted to consult a doctor, instead preferring attempts at spiritual healing. At last the Clemens' maid, Katy Leary, insisted on a doctor seeing Susy. The young woman, only 24, had spinal meningitis, which gradually left her delirious and then caused her to lose her sight before she entered a coma and passed away.

Twain, as he always did with the deaths of those he loved, felt personal responsibility for his daughter's death. He imagined that if he had not allowed himself to become ensnared in the financial troubles that necessitated the lecture tour, the family would have been together. He wrote his grief in letters to Livy, who, at the time, was still traveling across the Atlantic and was unaware of what had happened. Twain was unable to return to Elmira in time for Susy's burial.

After the funeral, Livy and the surviving two daughters sailed back to England. The family retired into seclusion, keeping their address in London mostly a secret. Christmas came before long—Susy's death had occurred in August—but the family did not mention the day or celebrate. In fact, they would celebrate few special days in the next couple of years—not Christmases, Thanksgivings, or even birthdays. Their grief was so deep that, according to Clara's account, a significant amount of time passed before anyone in the family laughed again.

Twain became more moody and bitter than ever before, writing of his deep resentment toward God in his essay, "In My Bitterness." He buried himself in writing, completing *Following the Equator* and revising it with Livy's editorial assistance, as always. The silence of the family, as the winter passed, gave rise to a rumor that Mark Twain had died. When a reporter appeared on his doorstep with instructions on how many words to write if he really was dead, Twain responded with one of his famous retorts: "You don't need as much as that. Just say the report of my death has been greatly exaggerated."

Still quite alive, Mark Twain and his family spent several years moving from place to place in Europe. He continued writing for hours every day, not even intending to publish much of what he wrote, but instead finding in the act of writing some respite from the "deadness" that he had felt since Susy's death. The family stayed in Vienna for a year so that Clara could work toward her ambition of a musical career—an ambition which neither of her parents approved of, but which they let her pursue nonetheless.

Twain finally succeeded in repaying all his debts, an accomplishment that not only brought him great peace of mind, but also one for which he was praised in newspapers around the globe. In Vienna, the family found themselves famous, respected, and sought-after by high society. Twain often liked to talk to reporters from the comfort of his favorite writing spot—his bed. During this time, he worked on two pieces, "The Chronicle of Young Satan" (that would become *The Mysterious Stranger*) and *What is Man?*, both of which develop Twain's views on the nature of humankind—that humanity's elevated place among the animals is unmerited and that a human is "merely a machine" with no real ability to act independently. Livy particularly disliked the second of these, which Twain did not publish until after her death.

Twain was eager to return home to the United States, but after two winters in Vienna for Clara's musical endeavors, Jean's health compelled the family to stay in Europe even longer. Jean had always been frail, and after Susy's death, she had begun to suffer from seizures. The family traveled to London and then to Sweden for the summer so that Jean could be treated by a Swedish doctor named Henrik Kellgren. Back in London, they lived in a country house called Dollis Hill, which Twain called "nearer to being paradise than any other home I ever occupied." But in the autumn of 1900, when Dr. Kellgren told the family that they could find a doctor in New York to work with Jean, Twain was delighted to be on his way back to America.

# Chapter Seven

# The Last Years

*"I came in with Halley's comet in 1835. It is coming again next year, and I expect to go out with it. It will be the greatest disappointment of my life if I don't go out with Halley's comet. The Almighty has said, no doubt: 'Now here are these two unaccountable freaks; they came in together, they must go out together.'"*

—Mark Twain, 1909

Life in New York was a swirl of activity as the United States welcomed back one of its most popular figures. Mark Twain was celebrated across the country. Reporters met the family at the boat, and it seemed as if they would never stop knocking on the door of the house the family subsequently rented.

Mark Twain now took the opportunity not just to reveal his mind through his fiction, but to speak out openly on a wide variety of topics. He had much to say about politics and was an especially outspoken critic of imperialism. As he now wrote passionately on sometimes-unpopular topics such as women's right to vote and the treatment of black Americans, he expected to lose popular support. Yet most of the public continued to revere him; Livy commented that the ratio of positive mail to negative was still "ten to one I should think." Twain declared that he would continue speaking his mind as long as Livy would let him.

Livy did not object to most of Twain's writings and opinions, but under the strain of their hectic life and the constant controversies, her health did begin to deteriorate. Twain moved the family to a home in quieter Riverdale, but they were still flooded with guests and incessantly busy. Jean's health had not improved, as she was still experiencing frequent seizures. Clara gave her debut musical performance in Washington, D.C. in 1901, and afterward insisted on going to Paris to study further despite her parents' objections. They were concerned about her living independently and living so near to the man she was in love with, the pianist Ossip Gabrilowitsch.

In the summer of 1902, Livy succumbed to the pressure and stress of all these events, suddenly struggling with heart and breathing problems. She and Twain both thought she was about to die. While Livy did not die, it was clear that the time had come for drastic action. Clara, back home from Paris, became her mother's caretaker, and Twain and Jean were barely allowed to see Livy. Livy and Twain missed each other and wrote notes back and forth. The following year, with Livy still resting in her bed, the family decided to sell the old house in Hartford; they saw now that they would never move back. By the summer of 1903, Livy was enough improved that she went with the family to Quarry Farm.

Livy once again took over managing the family, and on the advice of doctors, the family traveled to Florence for the winter. The warm weather of Italy was supposed to help Livy, but instead the strain of conflicts with their landlady combined with unexpectedly cold, damp weather took a further toll on her health, which grew steadily worse. Twain was sick as well, coming down with bronchitis and a lingering cough; he tried to cope by devoting himself to his writing and dictating an autobiography to his secretary, Isabel Lyon. Livy continued to edit Twain's writings. In February of 1904, Sam and Livy's 33rd wedding anniversary passed quietly; by this point, the family members were only allowed to see Livy briefly each day.

In Florence, Clara was caring for her mother and helping her father while also trying to further her musical career. Under the strain of all these responsibilities, she had a mental breakdown a few days after Twain and Livy's anniversary. She later wrote, "I don't know why I was so suddenly seized but at any rate I was seized by something & began to scream & curse & knocked down the furniture." She screamed that she hoped her family would die and threatened to kill them.

Clara's voice carried to her mother's room, where Livy suffered a heart attack. Though Clara recovered, Livy's health grew worse until June, when she suddenly seemed to be improving. She spent more time with the family at dinnertime, and after dinner Twain played the old spirituals on the piano that Livy and Susy had loved and that he had not played since Susy's death. As Sam played, Livy, listening from her bed upstairs, attended by the maid Kate Leary, quietly passed away.

Twain was left despondent and unable to make decisions, Clara blamed herself because of her previous breakdown, and Jean began to suffer from seizures again. Twain's secretary, Isabel Lyon, took charge and got the family, along with Livy's body, back home. There, things only grew worse as Clara's mental health deteriorated, and she soon checked herself into a sanatorium. Jean's seizures also grew worse, and she began to have fits of extreme violence, trying to kill Katy Leary, the family's maid, twice. Twain, feeling incapable of taking care of Jean, sent her to the first of several sanatoriums where she would remain for years.

In the depths of despair, Twain wrote in a letter the summer after Livy's death, "There is only empty space, and in it a lost and homeless and wandering and companionless and indestructible Thought. And . . . I am that thought."

When Clara left the sanatorium the following year, she lived with her father, yet the relationship between father and daughter became increasingly strained. They often antagonized or embarrassed one another, and consequently Clara often avoided Twain. Frequently lonely, Twain began friendships with a number of young girls who reminded him of his daughters in past days and who he described as grandchildren that he got to choose; he called these girls his "Angelfish."

Despite loneliness, Twain enjoyed his fame and the recognition he received everywhere he went. He was gratified to receive an honorary doctorate from Oxford in 1907—particularly because the applause for him lasted longer than for any of the other authors honored, who included famous figures like Rudyard Kipling.

Back in New York, however, Twain found his quiet and empty house depressing, calling it "The Valley of the Shadow." He bought a large piece of land in Connecticut, and Isabel Lyons, with Clara's help, worked with an architect to design a house there that recalled all the best times of Twain's life. It included details such as the mantelpiece from the house in Hartford. While Twain waited for the house to be built, he began going to Bermuda, where he found respite from all the demands on his time and attention.

In 1908, he moved into the new house, which he loved and named Stormfield. When tensions between Clara and Isabel Lyon rose, Clara demanded that he fire Isabel. Trying to preserve the last tatters of his relationship with Clara, Twain gave in. Without Isabel, he was left even more alone. So when Jean wrote asking to come home—not for the first time—Twain agreed.

He and Jean enjoyed getting to know each other again after their long separation; Jean was happy to care for her father, and Twain was surprised to find that Jean had "plenty of wisdom, judgment, penetration, [and] practical good sense—like her mother." In September of 1908, Clara at last married the man she had fallen in love with years before, Ossip Gabrilowitsch, whom she had also moved in with earlier. Twain, always eager for attention, wore his Oxford robes to the wedding. Clara and Ossip departed for Europe soon afterward, while Twain traveled to Bermuda again.

As Christmas approached and Twain returned to Stormfield, Jean did her best to recall the happy celebrations of earlier years with her decoration of the house. But then, on the morning of Christmas Eve, she had a seizure while in her bath. A heart attack evidently followed the seizure, and she was found dead by the maid, Katy Leary. Twain watched the hearse drive away from the house as Jean, Susy, and Livy's favorite music played. He then wrote the last manuscript he would finish, a chapter of his autobiography titled, "The Death of Jean."

Twain could no longer stand Stormfield without Jean, so he returned to Bermuda. There, his health began to fail. In April, Clara sailed to meet him and accompany him back to America. In Stormfield, she and her husband spent their days by her father's bedside. On the evening of April 21, 1910, Samuel Clemens, also known as Mark Twain, passed away in his sleep. As Clara would later write, "While the sun dimmed, the great soul of Mark Twain melted into that speechless state of majesty and calm he had so fervently yearned for."

# Conclusion

Ernest Hemingway once said, "All modern American literature comes from one book by Mark Twain called *Huckleberry Finn.*" Mark Twain's legacy certainly is a significant one. His keen observations of human nature, his sense of humor, and his prose style and use of vernacular language all helped to give unique direction to American literature, which had previously been considered an inferior imitation of British literature.

Though he is often remembered for his humor, Twain's serious side—in particular his unabashed willingness to engage with questions about slavery and race—is one of the most lastingly important aspects of his writing. His work pioneered the discussion of these issues that are still central to American literature. Even as he became bitter about life and disillusioned the nature of humanity, Samuel Clemens, through Mark Twain, wrote and worked for social good.

Samuel Clemens was a multi-faceted character, not an easy man to understand. Mark Twain, as an author who is both Clemens and an identity separate from Clemens, only adds to this. From this complex identity as both Clemens and Twain, from an adventurous and tragic life, and from observations of the world recorded with panache, humor, sometimes bitterness, and an ear for the distinctiveness of American English, came a complex and varied body of work which continues to be relevant to society today.

Made in United States
Orlando, FL
26 May 2025